Magical and Mythical Creatures

Cursive handwriting and activity workbook

Sophia Katy Platt

Instructions

Trace over the dashed lines
on the following pages to learn cursive.

Try writing the letters and words on your own
in the blank space.

Solve the puzzles.

Have fun!

Capital letters in cursive

A B C D E F G

H I J K L M N

O P Q R S T U

V W X Y Z

A B C D E F G

H I J K L M N

O P Q R S T U

V W X Y Z

Lowercase letters in cursive

a   b   c   d   e   f   g

h   i   j   k   l   m   n

o   p   q   r   s   t   u

v   w   x   y   z

a   b   c   d   e   f   g

h   i   j   k   l   m   n

o   p   q   r   s   t   u

v   w   x   y   z

a BCDEFGHIJKLMNOPQRSTUVWXYZ

A a

a a a a a a a a
a a a a a a a a
a a a a a a a a
a a a a a a a a a
a a a a a a a a a a
a a a a a a a a a a

Angel

a

a

a

a

Angel Angel Angel

Angel Angel Angel

Angel Angel Angel

Angel Angel Angel

Angel Angel Angel

angel angel angel

angel angel angel

angel angel angel

angel angel angel

angel angel angel

Angel glows and shines.

Angel glows and shines.

B b

B B B B B B B B B

B B B B B B B B B

B B B B B B B B B

b b b b b b b b b

b b b b b b b b b

b b b b b b b b b

Basilisk

B

B

b

b

Basilisk *Basilisk*

Basilisk *Basilisk*

Basilisk *Basilisk*

Basilisk *Basilisk*

Basilisk *Basilisk*

basilisk *basilisk*

basilisk *basilisk*

basilisk *basilisk*

basilisk *basilisk*

basilisk *basilisk*

Can you draw the Basilisk step-by-step?

Basilisk

ABCDEFGHIJKLMNOPQRSTUVWXYZ

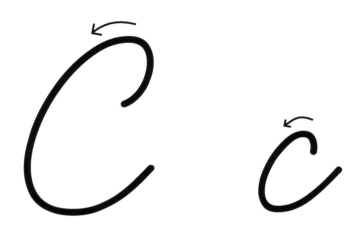

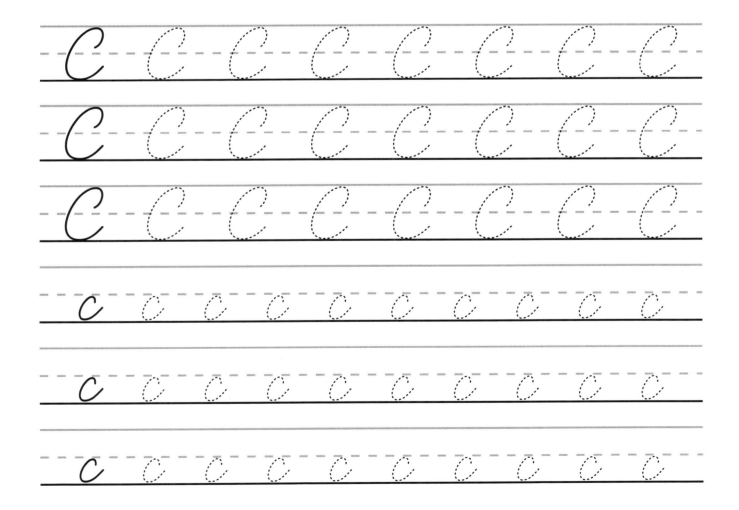

Cyclops

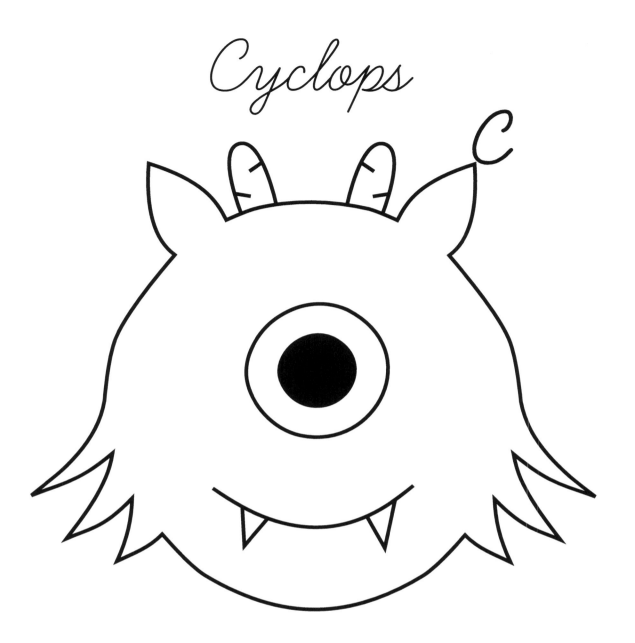

C

C

c

c

Cyclops *Cyclops*

Cyclops *Cyclops*

Cyclops *Cyclops*

Cyclops *Cyclops*

Cyclops *Cyclops*

cyclops *cyclops*

cyclops *cyclops*

cyclops *cyclops*

cyclops *cyclops*

cyclops *cyclops*

Connect the dots and draw the parts of the Cyclops' face!

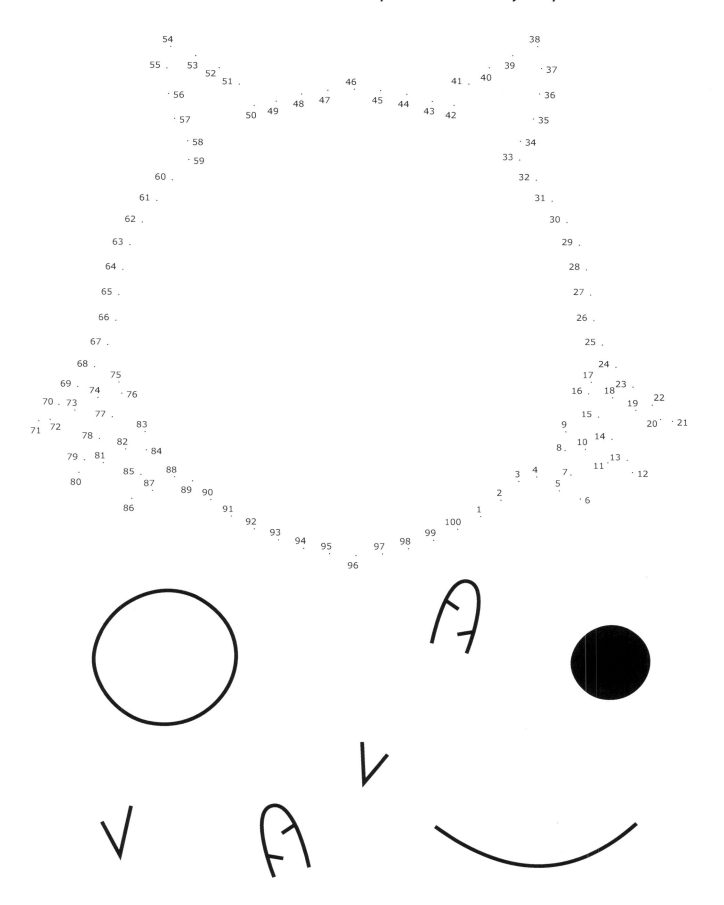

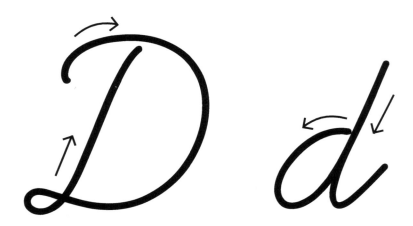

D D D D D D D D

D D D D D D D D

D D D D D D D D

d d d d d d d d d d d

d d d d d d d d d d d

d d d d d d d d d d d

Dragon

$\mathcal{D}$

$\mathcal{D}$

d

d

Dragon   Dragon

Dragon   Dragon

Dragon   Dragon

Dragon   Dragon

Dragon   Dragon

dragon   dragon

dragon   dragon

dragon   dragon

dragon   dragon

dragon   dragon

Dragon is hungry!

Dragon is hungry!

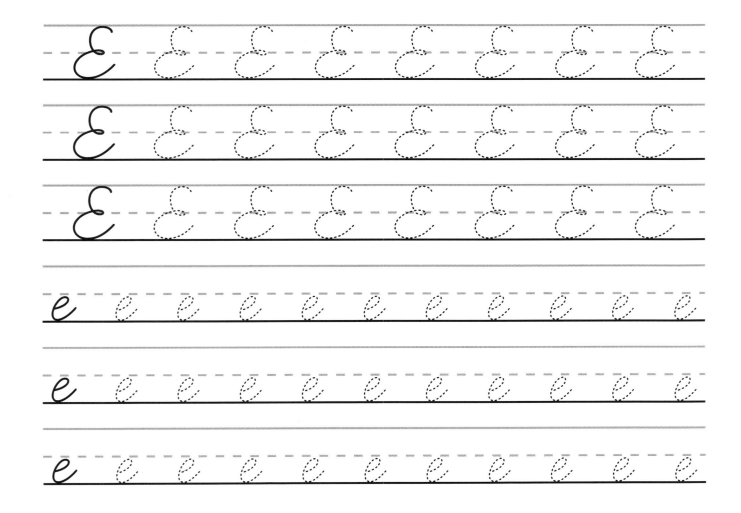

Elf

E --

E --

e --

e --

Elf   Elf   Elf   Elf   Elf

Elf   Elf   Elf   Elf   Elf

Elf   Elf   Elf   Elf   Elf

Elf   Elf   Elf   Elf   Elf

Elf   Elf   Elf   Elf   Elf

elf   elf   elf   elf   elf

elf   elf   elf   elf   elf

elf   elf   elf   elf   elf

elf   elf   elf   elf   elf

elf   elf   elf   elf   elf

Color the picture.

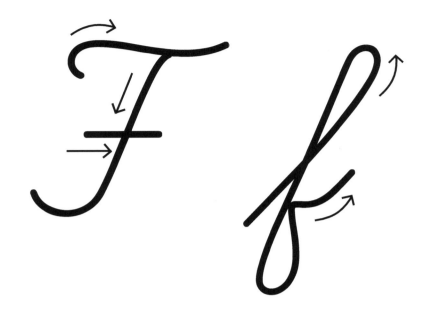

Fairy

$\mathcal{F}$ --

$\mathcal{F}$ --

f --

f --

Fairy   Fairy   Fairy

Fairy   Fairy   Fairy

Fairy   Fairy   Fairy

Fairy   Fairy   Fairy

Fairy   Fairy   Fairy

fairy   fairy   fairy   fairy

fairy   fairy   fairy   fairy

fairy   fairy   fairy   fairy

fairy   fairy   fairy   fairy

fairy   fairy   fairy   fairy

Do you remember the creature's names?

ABCDEF𝒢HIJKLMNOP2RSTUVWXY3

Goblin

G

G

g

g

Goblin Goblin Goblin

Goblin Goblin Goblin

Goblin Goblin Goblin

Goblin Goblin Goblin

Goblin Goblin Goblin

goblin goblin goblin

goblin goblin goblin

goblin goblin goblin

goblin goblin goblin

goblin goblin goblin

Can you draw the goblin step-by-step?

Goblin

ABCDEFG**H**IJKLMNOPQRSTUVWXYZ

H h

H H H H H H H H H H H H H

H H H H H H H H H H H H H

H H H H H H H H H H H H H

h h h h h h h h h h h h h

h h h h h h h h h h h h h

h h h h h h h h h h h h h

Hydra

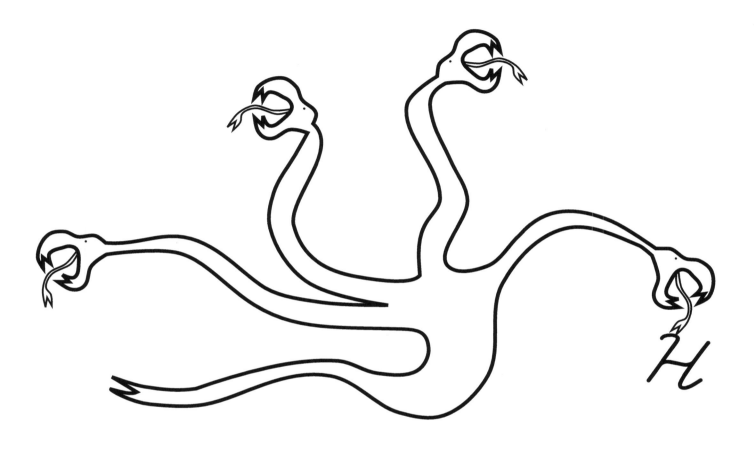

H

H

h

h

Hydra *Hydra* *Hydra*
Hydra *Hydra* *Hydra*
Hydra *Hydra* *Hydra*
Hydra *Hydra* *Hydra*
Hydra *Hydra* *Hydra*

hydra *hydra* *hydra*
hydra *hydra* *hydra*
hydra *hydra* *hydra*
hydra *hydra* *hydra*
hydra *hydra* *hydra*

The Hydra possessed

many heads.

The Hydra possessed

many heads.

ABCDEFGHIJKLMNOPQRSTUVWXYZ

$\mathcal{L}$ i

Ipotane

l

l

i

i

Ipotane   Ipotane

Ipotane   Ipotane

Ipotane   Ipotane

Ipotane   Ipotane

Ipotane   Ipotane

ipotane   ipotane

ipotane   ipotane

ipotane   ipotane

ipotane   ipotane

ipotane   ipotane

Let's trace and finish drawing the Ipotane.

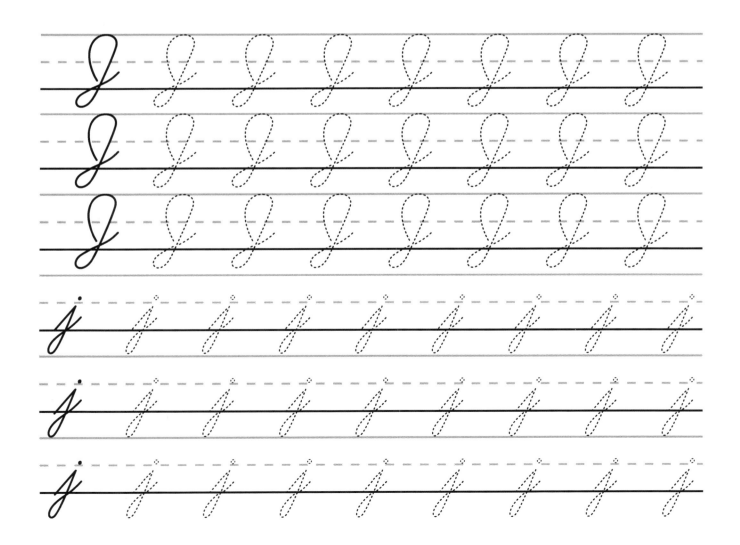

Jackalope

𝒥 ....

𝒥 ....

𝒿 ....

𝒿 ....

Jackalope Jackalope

Jackalope Jackalope

Jackalope Jackalope

Jackalope Jackalope

Jackalope Jackalope

jackalope jackalope

jackalope jackalope

jackalope jackalope

jackalope jackalope

jackalope jackalope

Find the way to the antlers.

ABCDEFGHIJ**K**LMNOPQRSTUVWXYZ

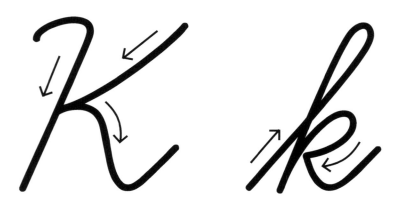

K K K K K K K K K K K K K

K K K K K K K K K K K K K

K K K K K K K K K K K K K

k k k k k k k k k k k k k

k k k k k k k k k k k k k

k k k k k k k k k k k k k

Karkinos

K --

K --

k --

k --

Karkinos   Karkinos

Karkinos   Karkinos

Karkinos   Karkinos

Karkinos   Karkinos

Karkinos   Karkinos

karkinos   karkinos

karkinos   karkinos

karkinos   karkinos

karkinos   karkinos

Karkinos is a giant crab.

Karkinos is a giant crab.

L l

L L L L L L L
L L L L L L L
L L L L L L L

l l l l l l l l l l
l l l l l l l l l l
l l l l l l l l l l

Leprechaun

$\mathscr{L}$

$\mathscr{L}$

ℓ

ℓ

Leprechaun Leprechaun

Leprechaun Leprechaun

Leprechaun Leprechaun

Leprechaun Leprechaun

Leprechaun Leprechaun

leprechaun leprechaun

leprechaun leprechaun

leprechaun leprechaun

leprechaun leprechaun

leprechaun leprechaun

Do you remember the creature's names?

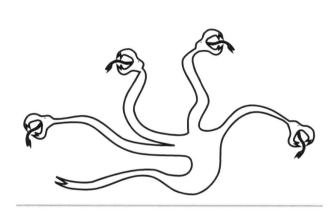

ABCDEFGHIJKLMNOPQRSTUVWXYZ

Mermaid

$\mathcal{M}$

$\mathcal{M}$

m

m

Mermaid _Mermaid_

Mermaid _Mermaid_

Mermaid _Mermaid_

Mermaid _Mermaid_

Mermaid _Mermaid_

mermaid _mermaid_

mermaid _mermaid_

mermaid _mermaid_

mermaid _mermaid_

mermaid _mermaid_

Let's trace and finish drawing the mermaid.

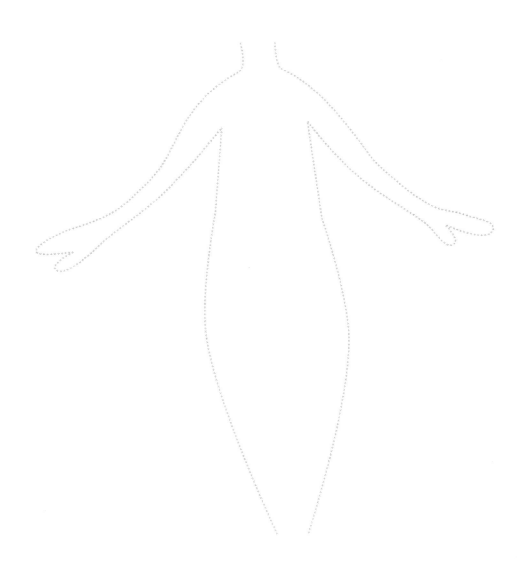

$\mathcal{N}$ $\mathcal{m}$

n n n n n n n

n n n n n n n

n n n n n n n

n m m m m m m m

n m m m m m m m

n m m m m m m m

Nymph

n   --------------------------------

n   --------------------------------

n   --------------------------------

n   --------------------------------

Nymph Nymph

Nymph Nymph

Nymph Nymph

Nymph Nymph

Nymph Nymph

nymph nymph nymph

nymph nymph nymph

nymph nymph nymph

nymph nymph nymph

nymph nymph nymph

Color the picture.

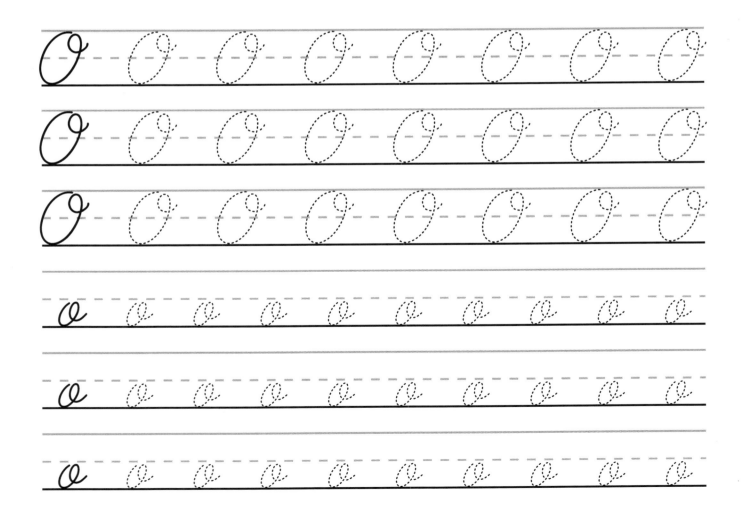

Ogre

$\mathcal{O}$

$\mathcal{O}$

$\mathcal{O}$

$\mathcal{O}$

Ogre Ogre Ogre Ogre

Ogre Ogre Ogre Ogre

Ogre Ogre Ogre Ogre

Ogre Ogre Ogre Ogre

Ogre Ogre Ogre Ogre

ogre ogre ogre ogre

ogre ogre ogre ogre

ogre ogre ogre ogre

ogre ogre ogre ogre

ogre ogre ogre ogre

Find the way to the machete.

$\mathcal{P}$ $\mathcal{P}$

$\mathcal{P}$ $\mathcal{P}$ $\mathcal{P}$ $\mathcal{P}$ $\mathcal{P}$ $\mathcal{P}$ $\mathcal{P}$ $\mathcal{P}$ $\mathcal{P}$ $\mathcal{P}$ $\mathcal{P}$

$\mathcal{P}$ $\mathcal{P}$ $\mathcal{P}$ $\mathcal{P}$ $\mathcal{P}$ $\mathcal{P}$ $\mathcal{P}$ $\mathcal{P}$ $\mathcal{P}$ $\mathcal{P}$ $\mathcal{P}$

$\mathcal{P}$ $\mathcal{P}$ $\mathcal{P}$ $\mathcal{P}$ $\mathcal{P}$ $\mathcal{P}$ $\mathcal{P}$ $\mathcal{P}$ $\mathcal{P}$ $\mathcal{P}$ $\mathcal{P}$

p p p p p p p p p p p

p p p p p p p p p p p

p p p p p p p p p p p

Pixie

$\mathcal{p}$

$\mathcal{p}$

$\mathcal{p}$

$\mathcal{p}$

Pixie *Pixie* *Pixie*

Pixie *Pixie* *Pixie*

Pixie *Pixie* *Pixie*

Pixie *Pixie* *Pixie*

Pixie *Pixie* *Pixie*

pixie *pixie* *pixie* *pixie*

pixie *pixie* *pixie* *pixie*

pixie *pixie* *pixie* *pixie*

pixie *pixie* *pixie* *pixie*

pixie *pixie* *pixie* *pixie*

Pixie is really little.

Pixie is really little.

ABCDEFGHIJKLMNOP**Q**RSTUVWXYZ

Q q

Q Q Q Q Q Q Q Q Q
Q Q Q Q Q Q Q Q Q
Q Q Q Q Q Q Q Q Q

q q q q q q q q q
q q q q q q q q q
q q q q q q q q q

Quinotaur

Q

Q

q

q

Quinotaur   Quinotaur

Quinotaur   Quinotaur

Quinotaur   Quinotaur

Quinotaur   Quinotaur

Quinotaur   Quinotaur

quinotaur   quinotaur

quinotaur   quinotaur

quinotaur   quinotaur

quinotaur   quinotaur

quinotaur   quinotaur

Find the correct shadow.

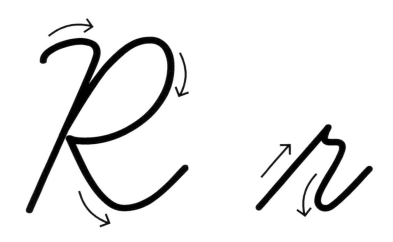

Roc

$\mathcal{R}$

$\mathcal{R}$

r

r

Roc   Roc   Roc   Roc

Roc   Roc   Roc   Roc

Roc   Roc   Roc   Roc

Roc   Roc   Roc   Roc

Roc   Roc   Roc   Roc

roc   roc   roc   roc   roc

roc   roc   roc   roc   roc

roc   roc   roc   roc   roc

roc   roc   roc   roc   roc

roc   roc   roc   roc   roc

Do you remember the creature's names?

ABCDEFGHIJKLMNOPQRSTUVWXYZ

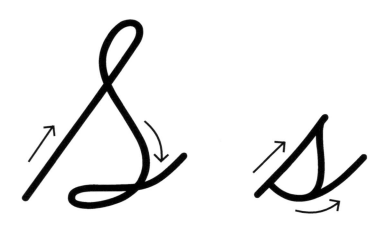

Squonk

$\mathcal{S}$ -

$\mathcal{S}$ -

s -

s -

Squonk *Squonk*

Squonk *Squonk*

Squonk *Squonk*

Squonk *Squonk*

Squonk *Squonk*

squonk *squonk squonk*

squonk squonk squonk

squonk squonk squonk

squonk squonk squonk

squonk squonk squonk

Can you draw the squonk step-by-step?

1

2

3

4

Squonk

T t

T T T T T T T T

T T T T T T T T

T T T T T T T T

t t t t t t t t

t t t t t t t t

t t t t t t t t

Troll

$\mathcal{T}$

$\mathcal{T}$

t

t

Troll Troll Troll
Troll Troll Troll
Troll Troll Troll
Troll Troll Troll
Troll Troll Troll

troll troll troll troll
troll troll troll troll
troll troll troll troll
troll troll troll troll
troll troll troll troll

Trolls love mountains.

Trolls love mountains.

A B C D E F G H I J K L M N O P Q R S T u V W X Y Z

Unicorn

U

U

U

u

u

Unicorn Unicorn

Unicorn Unicorn

Unicorn Unicorn

Unicorn Unicorn

Unicorn Unicorn

unicorn unicorn

unicorn unicorn

unicorn unicorn

unicorn unicorn

unicorn unicorn

Find the way to the horn.

V

v

Vampire

$\mathscr{V}$

$\mathscr{V}$

$\mathscr{v}$

$\mathscr{v}$

Vampire Vampire

Vampire Vampire

Vampire Vampire

Vampire Vampire

Vampire Vampire

vampire vampire

vampire vampire

vampire vampire

vampire vampire

vampire vampire

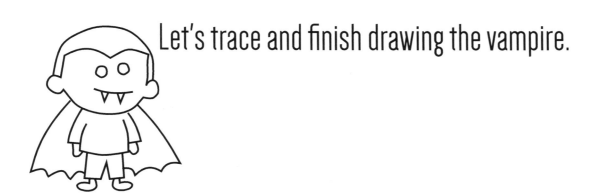 Let's trace and finish drawing the vampire.

Wani

W

W

w

w

Wani Wani Wani

Wani Wani Wani

Wani Wani Wani

Wani Wani Wani

Wani Wani Wani

wani wani wani

wani wani wani

wani wani wani

wani wani wani

wani wani wani

Wani lives in water.

Wani lives in water.

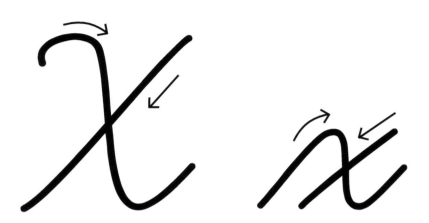

Xelhua

𝒳

𝒳

𝓍

𝓍

Xelhua *Xelhua*

Xelhua *Xelhua*

Xelhua *Xelhua*

Xelhua *Xelhua*

Xelhua *Xelhua*

xelhua *xelhua* *xelhua*

xelhua *xelhua* *xelhua*

xelhua *xelhua* *xelhua*

xelhua *xelhua* *xelhua*

xelhua *xelhua* *xelhua*

Color the picture.

ABCDEFGHIJKLMNOPQRSTUVWXYZ

Yy Y Y Y Y Y Y Y Y

Y Y Y Y Y Y Y Y Y

Y Y Y Y Y Y Y Y Y

y y y y y y y y y

y y y y y y y y y

y y y y y y y y y

Yeti

𝒴

𝒴

𝓎

𝓎

Yeti Yeti Yeti

Yeti Yeti Yeti

Yeti Yeti Yeti

Yeti Yeti Yeti

Yeti Yeti Yeti

yeti yeti yeti yeti

yeti yeti yeti yeti

yeti yeti yeti yeti

yeti yeti yeti yeti

yeti yeti yeti yeti

Yeti is a large creature.

Yeti is a large creature.

Zombie

𝒵
𝒵
𝒵
𝒵

Zombie Zombie

Zombie Zombie

Zombie Zombie

Zombie Zombie

Zombie Zombie

zombie zombie

zombie zombie

zombie zombie

zombie zombie

zombie zombie

Do you remember the creature's names?

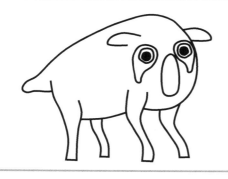

Thank you!

Made in the USA
Middletown, DE
12 December 2022

18348625R00062